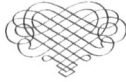

Her journey ... finding anew, a SELF ... exploring the inner realms of Spirit, the vistas of Eternal quest, the depths of Love, and the Freedom to BE, to BE her own Birth Eternal ... her words, a dialogue with the pulsing of heart, with the vision of light, with the embrace of truth, known and so endearingly put forth ... yes, her journey ... finding anew, a SELF.

–*Rose Marie Raccioppi, MS FABI*
Poet Laureate
Orangetown, New York

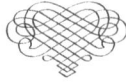

Char knows what adversity is. From the moment Char was born, her mother rejected her. In her lifetime, she has been diagnosed with breast cancer four times, was diagnosed as legally blind, was voted the top attorney in her state, only to lose her practice after diagnosis, got divorced, became a single parent, and lost her home that she had created as her sanctuary.

These life challenges taught Char how to tap into that unshakable power that we all have, and she shows you in this book how you can tap into this amazing source of resiliency, rebirth, and truth for yourself.

–Beverly Vote
Publisher, Breast Cancer Wellness Magazine

In an authentic and engaging voice, Char leads us through her journey of reconciliation of her past with the resultant discovery of self-love and personal power. Readers will find inspiration, hope, and guidance with these transferable lessons in the establishment of their own legacies. Char's impassioned purpose to truly make a difference in the world is apparent and impactful.

–Susan Sember
Film Director & Producer
Silverlight Films, LLC

UNSHAKEABLE POWER
Through Seasons of the Soul

Printed and Electronic Versions
ISBN: 978-1-7340250-2-6
(Charlotte Murphy /Motivation Champs)

Cover photo credit: Skip Thomas

The book was printed
in the United States of America.

To order additional copies or bulk order contact the publisher, Motivation Champs Publishing. www.motivationchamps.com

Acknowledgments

This path my life has taken up until now has brought many successes, much love, and some bitter pain and disappointments.

Throughout all of it, I choose now to focus on the people, the beautiful souls who encouraged me to keep going, believed in me wholeheartedly, prayed in earnest for me, and at times, literally picked me up and said, "Go for it; you can do this!" You all cheered me on, saying, "You got this too. Keep going!"

You're the ones who held my hand in doctor appointments, sat through all my surgeries, drove me to treatments for months at a time, changed my bandages, dressed me, fed me, and watched over me. And to you, I want to say "Thank you." I'm so very grateful for you all being in my life.

The list is extensive, and I can't list you all here, but

you know who you are. (Smile.)

My mom and dad, who did their very best to raise me to be the best I could possibly be, who sacrificed and gave me every opportunity to succeed in life.

Chris Brown, my only child who turned out to be my hero; the best son, friend, husband, and dad anyone could ever want.

My first-grade teacher, Suzanne McGee, who stood up for me when it became apparent I was left-handed and different from the rest, believed that I would do just fine growing up as a 'leftie.'

The people who helped and contributed to this book becoming 'real' and not just a figment of my imagination:

My dear friends Todd George Stone, Susan Sember, Beverly Vote, Susan Menanno, James Stewart, Jenna Jumonville Janisch, Jerry C. Hulsey, Anthony Sergio, Rose Marie Raccioppi, Jackie Hartsell Mallott, and last but certainly not least, Dominick Domasky—my devoted, motivating, and talented publisher.

And as I said, so many, many, more.

I am forever grateful and I love each and every single one of you.

Char Murphy

UNSHAKEABLE POWER
Through Seasons of the Soul

By
Charlotte Murphy

SEASONS OF THE SOUL

I've been through the winters of my soul;
layered up, hiding inside.
Protecting myself from the dangerous,
relentless elements pursuing me.
Yet, I had to be exposed enough to breathe
and see to experience the elements of a
cruel season;
filled with empty, cold, dead and many
dark days.
The season targets where and when it can;
killing off anything exposed, as that is just
the nature of the storm itself;
doing its job in spite of any obstacles
placed innocently in its path.
Yet, I remind myself of one thing:
it's merely just a

SEASON.

A soul's journey of endings and renewal;
a new season is on its way, bringing with
it new

BEGINNINGS.

Offering a new life, an old life renewed;
I remind myself,
there is no hope
without experiencing total loss;
no true joy
without profound sadness;
no faith without doubt;
and absolutely no resurrection
without

A DEATH.

I allowed the bitter season to kill off
what it needed to;
laying my hope and faith at my feet,
knowing that no suffering shall be in vain.
And I await ... till I see the first sign of light;
of green, the first bud, and then finally,
the first

BLOOM.

The new season of my soul reminds me;

the sun, the light ... that the dark clouds
had been hiding ...

Have been there all along.

And a new season of life begins again.

Todd George-Stone 1-23-18

Contents

Foreword

She has touched the heart and soul of many ...
through her own life experiences ... ups and downs,
wins and losses ... those who were lost on their life's
path, not knowing which way to turn, which direction to take, asking ... "Who AM I now?" "Who am
I?" "Why am I here?" "What's my purpose?"

She, the compassionate, embodiment of "The Angel
of Hope," shining her beacon of light on the wound-
ed warrior's untapped, dark space between heart and
mind ... a "soul whisperer," a power-filled survivor
"encourager of people," guide, mentor, a born leader
...
empowering, inspiring, and motivating to "rise up by
diving deep" ... within ...
to re-create, re-ignite, resurrect ... the inner voice dying to be heard, courage, truth, self-love, and respect
... to live authentically, living passions and dreams
through a renewed sense of self ... confidence, faith,
and trust in your higher power ... ending with a sense
of peace and freedom to truly "BE" the YOU you
were created to "Be"... the YOU you've always been
but couldn't find ... and to live in gratitude for it ALL
... knowing those were the places you had to go to

witness the true power ... within.

Anthony Sergio
Co-Founder Natural Nirvana

RE-IGNITE YOUR PURPOSE, PASSIONS, AND INNER TRUTHS

Introduction

My life's mission and true purpose and joy is and always has been to bless others, as I have been blessed. To inspire, empower, and encourage the masses with my message of hope, love, kindness, and faith. To touch as many hearts as possible from my heart ... teaching, speaking, authoring books and magazine articles. I receive my greatest rewards in life by sharing experiences from my incredible journey of "survival" dodging bullets to healing and "thriving" as the authentic ME ... I help YOU to heal; find your peace, joy, inner power; and discover your deepest desires. My greatest goal is to uplift you, to help you heal from your past, to love and embrace yourself through life's many challenges. I teach you how to go from asking "Why me?" to learning and growing through sharing my life's experiences and embracing life as it presents itself. And to live in a constant state of gratitude for ALL of it. To "find and live the real you." Knowing you're better than okay, YOU ARE AMAZING! YOU are enough. I always say, "Love and believe in yourself, with all your scars; just be you; keep going and never give up on living your truth, purpose, passions, and dreams."

I, like you, my friends, have asked for answers to all those soul-burning questions ... searching desperately, everywhere for the answers. Yet, frustratingly, not immediately finding them. I have been lost on the winding, bumpy, uphill trek of life many times ... confused, uncertain about what the future held and crying out for help. I was frozen in that time and space of unknowingness.

Yes, at one point or another, haven't we all been there? Are you at a crossroad in your life, not knowing which way is north, south, east, or west and certainly unsure of which direction would take you to where?

It's time the truth be revealed. To find you, your clarity of purpose, know with confidence which direction you are going, and why you are going there. Believing without doubt; no more fear, questioning, overthinking, or halfway committing to the truths of who you are and why you are here now.

These are not really secrets; they are revelations. Revelations of that which may not be forefront in your mind at the moment because you have only temporarily forgotten, hidden them deep within. We are all here on this journey together to rediscover who we are as individuals and as a whole. We are

constantly recreating ourselves in every moment of our existence. You are a new creation in every minute of time. You are not the same as you were even one second ago.

Awakening to these truths of who you really are ... is a remembrance of long-known underpinnings of a reality we each have known all along, just not fully realized or tapped into as of yet. Are you living in darkness, behind a mask to cover your light?

My purpose is to help remind you and to give you some tools, which you can use to uncover your truth and power, your "inner alchemist." To transform and create the life you were meant to live. To remove the mask, come out of hiding ... fully stepping up and into your light. The light that is you.

In these pages, I'm going to uncover some hidden gems of these truths—by sharing some insight into my journey on this path of life through the whirl-wind of changes, challenges, the roller coaster that brought me to the here and now. How I found my inner power, peace, truth, and light to help heal and guide you to gain some understanding, knowledge, and clarity; for you to fully and completely step into the greatest version of you.

Please now take my hand; let's walk this path together as one, with the *all* that is.

And discover the wonders, the magic of *you* that lie buried within. Buried in the rubble of your past. Revelations that are the truths and power of you. Bringing to you the life you truly deserve and have been promised. Shall we delve deeper? Come let's go now.

CHAPTER 1

Being in Darkness

Have you been ignoring you? Hiding from yourself and others? Are you living in the dark? Concealed behind some false mask of who you really are? Let's admit it ...We all have done it. Admitting that fact and facing it head-on with truth and integrity is critical for self-awareness and growth. And I hear you saying, "Yes ... but how do I do that?"

This vision occurred to me about life on the street.

A dangerous and dark street where all temptations and the ugliness of life in the dark really looked like ... I was terrified about what was going on all around me. It felt so unsafe and immeasurably fearful that I could not stay in that darkest-of-the-dark place. I was scared. I wanted to go home, to the home I grew up in. But no one was there anymore. It was dark and

empty, void of light and life. *Where was I? Where was I going? Who am I?* I knew not the answers.

Negative, fearful thoughts, feelings, and emotions were pouring throughout my soul. Keeping me a prisoner of my past. I was caught unaware. In the dark all alone. These questions haunting me day and night. Circling, spinning out of control in my mind. *Was this a figment of my imagination? Is this my destiny?*

I, somehow, by the Grace of God, was lifted out of the shadow of death by angels. I felt a gentle tug at my heart, a soft voice from deep inside my soul, reminding me of who I AM.

I listened in silence for days, months, still questioning, but as time slowly passed by ... I began to see a glimmer of hope, a sign of new life. Putting it all together one day, one step at a time.

As the distinguished Wayne Dyer said many times, "You are a spark of the Divine." An aha moment ... I, me, including all of my little quirks and imperfections, was born into this life, created to become more than that which had been haunting me. More than my past programming, more than my fears, more than my thoughts and emotions. I had been gifted dreams to fulfill and a joy-filled purpose suited

uniquely for me. I was gently reminded, pushed forward to learn to love, value, and accept myself fully for everything I am. And to change the things I could and not beat myself up for the things I couldn't. To stop living the lies I had been told, to step out of the dark fully, and finally to embrace the light of the real me.

I could not change the past, but I certainly learned a lot from it. And those lessons were of value. I keep them with me always.

I realized that I had hidden my light from everyone, including myself, for far too long. And by doing so, I was living in the shadows of my own truth. Not allowing my light to shine. It was time to release myself from the bonds of my past, to shift my paradigm, to energetically live my passions and dreams; to re-ignite my purpose for living and still always to honor and be true to myself. To know in my heart that I am enough.

CHAPTER 2

What is a Paradigm?

Paradigm is a mental program that has almost exclusive control over our habitual behavior … and almost all of our behavior is habitual.

Paradigms are a multitude of habits passed down from generation to generation.

Paradigms are the way you view yourself, the world, and opportunity.

Paradigms are how you approach change and challenges.

–Bob Proctor

Everyone has different conditioning in life by certain

persons, religions, life circumstances in general; they all play a huge part in this definition of who we are or who we think we are. Everyone has a totally different past. The mistake we make when it comes to understanding who we really are is, we believe that our conditions in life, our past, our shortcomings, our circumstances are what define us. They don't. Those are the lies, the excuses we fall back on to stay stuck there—in our mind. *I'm not strong enough; I'm not good enough; I'm not smart; I'm not thin enough ...* those are the recordings in our head that we replay over and over and over again until they become who we think we are; the mind believes that which we feed it. And as a result, we become that which we aren't. Or that which we tell ourselves we are.

It's time to shred those old, worn-out recordings, to throw them out with the trash that they are. And to start playing brand new recordings; feeding our mind positive, loving, pleasing vibes and thoughts. Re-creating the image of who we are by changing our thoughts, thereby changing our lives. That is the alchemy of life, the power that you own. It's there for everyone to tap into; no one is left out. You have this ability within you right now.

CHAPTER 3

How Our Life's Conditioning Controls Us

My conditioning in life came partly in the way I was raised and the circumstances I created around this — by believing the lies of who I was told that I was and what I should or shouldn't do. I never knew what it felt like to just be me.

Never was I encouraged to love and accept myself as being enough just the way I am. Always having to prove myself to someone. To be who they thought I should be. To live up to their expectations of me and what I was told I should do. Never believing I was even pretty, but certainly not pretty enough. I was never smart enough, never good enough, always too this or not enough of that. Constantly trying to please everyone else, never myself. How dare I? That would be selfish. I was never deserving of unconditional

love from others just the way I am. I always had to be someone else.

Are you believing these lies? It's really easy to fall into that trap. To be depressed and anxious. Feeling alone, scared, and unloved.

Many different things can contribute to these feelings.

Now, I know who I am. Seeing my future, feeling it, breathing it, creating it, and manifesting it into reality. It was a tough part of my journey through life to get here to this point. We must choose to remember who we are and why we're here and to totally accept, love, and believe in ourselves and all that we are.

I have had failures that were hidden from even myself. I could not accept and overcome them, as they had been hidden by fear and shame so deep and for so long in the darkness within. I was still stuck in the old beliefs and patterns, living the paradigm of my past. I couldn't face these failures because they were just more proof to myself that I was just not enough.

Breaking through these walls that seemed unshakeable was not easy but well worth the trials, the fires, the dark pits of what felt like hell I had to move

through to get to the light, to see and live the reality of me. The real, authentic me.

Now, having gone through the process of recovering, healing from all I've been through in my life, some of which I will share here, required digging deep down inside my heart and searching my soul. Bringing back into the light who I know now that I am.

Through all of the layers upon layers of trauma from abuse, pain, abandonment and rejection, dealing with each and every negative thought and emotion as they came up, I finally became clear ... that I am who I am.

And the me that I AM is a beautiful soul, a strong and mighty spirit that shines her light on whoever she encounters in even the smallest of ways. She's resilient, kind with a heart of gold. Nothing can stop her; she is unshakeable as a spark of the Divine.

And nothing or no one will ever be able to take that truth away from her. This is what I believe we all are searching desperately to find. I am here to help you break through these paradigms, to shed the masks, creep slowly out of the darkness, and come fully into the light as the being of enlightenment that you truly are.

CHAPTER 4

Revealing the Light, Dropping the Mask

Are you hiding in the dark behind a mask which you believe is acceptable to someone else? I sure was. What or who are you wearing a mask to protect yourself from? You see, we all wear masks at times to cover up our own truths. And we hide in the dark behind them, afraid to shine our own light. Why? Because someone might not like us? Someone might reject us?

We judge and blame others sometimes through our whole lives to hide from who we really are. I'll reveal in these pages the revelations behind the *why*, and you will see through the "blind spots." You actually are hiding from yourself the truth of who you are.

We cover up and protect ourselves from being seen

fully in our light. We can do this in many different ways.

A lot of times, we bury our light, our authenticity of who and what we are, so deep within that we can't see it or even believe it's there. It's hidden in the blind spot of our mind's eye. Hiding in the ashes of our past. We are living our paradigm.

What were or are the circumstances in your life that convinced you on such a deep level that you're not good enough; that you're not beautiful, smart, capable, and worthy and are just plain doomed to be a failure? Are you in pain over it?

We use alcohol, drugs, anything to numb this pain, and we don't even know why we do it. We know it's not right, but we just keep doing it anyway.

These are some of the masks we wear that temporarily hide the pain, let us hide behind whatever our drug of choice is. But these are fake and temporary cover-ups and will fail us over time and also can and will kill us if we allow this to continue. It's an illusion created in our mind that we are safe and hidden there in the dark behind the masks we have created for protection from mostly our very own selves.

Is that what you are doing to hide from yourself and everyone else? To squelch your emotions and deny yourselves the freedom to shine your light unto the world?

I see; I understand. My 2020 vision has been restored. I took the mask off.

CHAPTER 5

My Life's Journey

Let me revert to my history growing up. And you may be able to relate to some or all of it.

I was the firstborn to a narcissistic socialite who was the only girl in a family of three boys during the depression era. Her mother was a widow; her father deceased before she was born. He was the owner of the Mercantile in England, Arkansas, during the early 1900s. He left my grandmother enough money to raise the four children and provide for their education without worry during a very tumultuous time in history when others were not faring too well.

My mother went to a prestigious all-girls college, Tulane's Sophie Newcomb, and was voted Junior

Favorite by her peers. She was a decorated beauty by all accounts and a "sorority girl." She received her degree in teaching but never used it until after my father died.

My father was born to a couple who were divorced a short time later. His mother, my grandmother, grew up on a farm outside Dayton, Ohio, and worked hard all her life just to make ends meet. Her life during the depression was not so easy. She later remarried, and the family grew to five children, and she divorced again. She almost lost her children because being a two-time divorcée, which was highly frowned upon back then, she could not take care of them. The church, however, stepped in to help her, and she was able to keep the family together.

My father, on the other hand, worked hard from an early age and was the only one of his siblings to graduate from college. He graduated from Ohio State University and went straight into the US Navy, which paid for his education in accounting. He later received his CPA; he made his living by that trade.

So, you can by now clearly see what happened here. There weren't many professional men back then, but my father was. Young, successful in his own right, and handsome as well. He had moved to Arkan-

sas from Ohio to take a job with a large company and met my mother on a blind date. He was a good "catch."

They subsequently fell in love and married a short time later. Four years afterward, I was born. My middle brother, two years after; the youngest eight years later.

My father worked to give my mother the life she was used to having and to give us the life he never had.

The marriage was a very strained one; my mother expected everything and had never taken care of anyone before. My father was the breadwinner and the caretaker of all of us.

My mother rejected me, her only girl, because she thought I was a fat baby and did not belong to her from the second she laid eyes on me. She even went as far as not feeding me for years so I wouldn't be fat. I was not her ideal daughter and never would be until I went to law school and became a successful attorney.

My parents became physically and mentally abusive toward each other from the first I can remember. It was terrifying to me, as I would hear them fighting,

and I was neglected, being left in the daybed behind bars, crying for help, hungry and wet.

The fighting would continue, even until my father died from ALS at the young age of 54.

During those times of screaming and fighting with each other at night when I was a teenager, my mother would come to my window in her gown and robe, on the front side of the house in one of the most prestigious neighborhoods in Little Rock at the time. She would knock hard on the window, crying and begging for me to come let her back in the house because my father had locked her out.

Well, there was no way I could leave my bedroom and walk past the living room where my father was to go let my mother back in, no matter how much I wanted to help her. This continued night after night until I went away to college at 18.

I wanted to help both of them for most of my life, but I couldn't save them from themselves, and I felt guilty about this. We never really can save anyone; only they can do that. But we can save ourselves— and only ourselves. It's a personal choice, like everything else in life.

I wanted, from a very young age, to help them both somehow, and I felt like a failure not to be able to help them or my father when he was dying from ALS.

Ironically, or not, I was finally able to help my mother recently, as she lay bedridden and dying, with advanced-stage Alzheimer's. Funny how she knew I would give her the best, even to my own detriment. She had made me Power of Attorney over her health care.

I was made to feel too fat, not smart enough, not pretty enough by my mother my whole life. She wanted me to be a debutante like she was, but I wasn't, nor ever would be.

I, again, felt like a total disappointment. The truth is, I wasn't fat; I was pretty, and I was smart, but I was never told this.

I was a daddy's girl, though, and he enjoyed buying me pretty clothes when I was young. This made my mother mad and extremely jealous. So, I became the object of her frustrations. I remember my father telling her one day that I would never be able to forgive her for what she was doing to me. But I had no idea why he would say that.

It only became clear to me much later in life. Growing up, I felt totally worthless, not being able to help either one of them. I was just never good enough, and I began to not like myself.

My father did instill something very strong in me from a young age that has stuck with me and has been my "saving grace" through all these years.

That is, "If you believe you can do something, and you want to do it bad enough, you can and will do it."

It sounds very simple, but it is a powerful principle that I write about often. Through all I've encountered in my life, that is perhaps the strongest thing that got me to see past everything in my blind spots and to enable me to keep moving forward.

What occurred from all of this is, I continuously felt unworthy in my relationships with men and even with friends. I never felt accepted or loved for who I am. And it's taken years of abuse, abuse from others and self-abuse, rejection of myself and by others, repeated serious illnesses, broken relationship after broken relationship to put this all together.

Not feeling loved or being able to love myself, not

taught self-love, rather guilt for not being able to take care of or do enough to help anyone, I retreated many times into darkness, where I was hiding from myself, hiding the light within me, always wearing a mask to try and be something or someone else to please and save everyone.

Eventually, going to law school and becoming a successful attorney was about helping and pleasing others and to feel successful in my life—a mask I wore to cover up who I really was and do what was really in my heart.

My father was deceased when I went back to law school, but it was to please him, as I had always tried to do, as well as make my mother like me and accept me, which she finally did—because, you see, I was making her look good. Look who she had created.

So, I was helping lots of people and pleasing my parents, and people wanted to be my friend because I was successful and well known. Finally, I had done something right.

However, all that would come to a screeching halt. After 15 years of practicing law, wearing the mask of a false identity that I had created made me sick.

I was diagnosed with breast cancer the first time at the height of my career at age 48, just after being voted "Best Lawyer" in Central Arkansas.

And then three more breast cancer recurrences on top of that. Then the mastectomy. I was no longer able to take care of my business, my finances, or myself. I had given it all away, trying to please others and help everyone else.

Ironically, the same thing happened to my father. He was a successful CPA with his own firm when diagnosed with ALS. He could no longer provide for or take care of himself or his family. So many parallels; it's eerie. I didn't literally die, yet in a sense, I did. I died to myself, but my father did die. I was the blessed one.

Years after I lost everything, and I do mean everything, including a newly remodeled dream home, my career, the "identity" of who I thought was me as a successful attorney, my marriage to whom I thought was my soul mate. I lost my path, my passion, the self-worth I had built up wearing the lawyer mask. It had only served me temporarily to cover up the real me.

I had no idea what I was going to do or how I would

make it. A repetition of so many other junctures in my life.

I, again, felt helpless, worthless; a failure, a disaster. I blamed myself but was only doing what I was told to do, or what I thought was right in order to make others happy and like me.

My family, including my mother, pretty much wrote me off, not understanding why I couldn't practice law anymore. Not even acknowledging or helping me through my repetitive illnesses or the double mastectomy. Even those who I thought were my friends disappeared, as well as my husband whom I adored.

I became depressed, anxious, engulfed with sadness and confusion, not knowing who I was, questioning myself about why I had even been saved. I shut myself off, turned off my inner light, and drowned myself in the darkness of alcohol, self-loathing, and self-pity, temporarily numbing, hiding the pain within my broken heart and soul.

What saved me and why? After years of not knowing I was so miserable, I was in a state of self-abuse, starving myself of even food because I still thought I was too fat ... yes, it was me doing it to me, not

my mother now. I was blinded from seeing myself, literally, as I later became legally blind. I underwent five eye surgeries in one year to regain my sight, and I suddenly no longer had a "blind spot." All became very clear to me.

I was spared for a reason. I'd always known I had a higher purpose in my life, but I had lost sight of what that was. I spent years in therapy, on disability, trying to figure it all out. I was totally in my head, not my heart. My mind had been allowed to take over by me. Thinking, feeling, totally believing the negative thoughts, the lies which overwhelmed and consumed me and I was allowing to control me.

I finally started digging inside myself, looking for the answers. But before this internal work and healing began, I had been thinking the whole time they would all be found *outside* of me, being ignorant of the truth that the answers I had been seeking, were buried deep inside of me. That's where the real me had been hidden all along. And realizing that one fact saved my life and allowed me to fully step out and up into my inner power; living my purpose, passions, and truths.

All I knew was, I had always wanted to write and speak, to help as many people any way I could. I

began to go deeper inside, to see a glimmer of hope within. My light was starting to sparkle more and more. I started to see a bigger picture of who I AM and what my true purpose was, and always had been.

And then suddenly it dawned on me. I had been given these *gifts* in the form of pain and hardships, blessed with all of it to give me the opportunity to do *more* to *help* others who might be going through what I had been through! Wow! What a beautiful revelation. That was it! I had awakened to my own truth.

I began to go deeper inside, to see a glimmer of hope within. My light was starting to sparkle more and more. I started to see a bigger picture of who I AM and what my true purpose was, and always had been. I was being resurrected by the light to a brand-new vision, newfound strength to live that purpose I knew I was brought here and saved for.

My passion for life was returning as I shed the masks I had been hiding behind, no longer caring what others thought.

I know now, hindsight really is 2020. I had to forgive myself for everything I had control over but had allowed unconsciously to happen and then forgive

everyone else I had been blaming. And once this was done, I could step fully into my true essence and the fullness of the power of who I AM, the authentic me, no longer hiding in the ashes of my past. I AM free; my heart is full of love for me, and I can say it out loud, not ashamed of anything about myself any longer.

I AM who I AM, and no one can ever take that away from me again.

Don't be fearful of your own shadows. Come out of the dark and into the light where you belong. Shed your masks and step into your full power, passion, and purpose. It's what you're here to do, just like me. We're no different. We just have differences in the way our greatness, our light is brought to the fore-front. You are your inner light; you are love; you are your heart, not your mind. You are enough, and you need to know it.

I AM blessed, grateful for it all, to be able to be here now to tell you this and to empower and inspire you to shed the masks that you're hiding behind and find the light, the gems lying dormant, hidden deep inside you once again. To give you hope to find your bliss and to live your joy.

To live your passions, purpose, and greatest dreams. This is what you deserve, and it's the secret revelation of why we are all here.

"You can do it if you only just believe you can and want to do it bad enough."

Sometimes, you just have to start all over! And that means purging the past from your mind, only holding on to what you've learned. Put the rest behind you and move on, no matter what that means or how hard it feels or what it looks like to you.

With hard work, belief in yourself, and determination, know that you can and will do it.

And then do it! You can make a better life for yourself and your loved ones.

Know that *you are worthy* of love and all things wonderful.

You are worthy to have abundance in all forms. Yes! You are worthy!

Live your dreams. Only you are in control of making the decisions and taking the steps necessary to make this happen.

Mantras for a New Paradigm

Daily mantras for a joy-filled, worry-free, guilt-free, and successful life: Living your passions, purpose, and dreams.

*I AM worthy and deserve to be loved and to fully live all my dreams, passions, and purpose.

*I choose to leave the past in the past, only taking with me the lessons I have learned.

*I choose to forgive myself and have a life free of guilt over anything I have done in the past.

*I choose to forgive others and to take full responsibility for myself and my actions or inactions.

*I choose to be free of worry over my future, as I know that all things work together for good.

*I choose to always live in the present moment of now.

*I choose to believe that everything that happens in my life is for a reason and moves me further toward my life's purpose.

*I AM worthy and deserve peace, love, joy, and all things good.

*I AM fulfilled and happy in the now, grateful for everything that has gotten me to where I AM now.

*It's my destiny to live my greatest desires, dreams, and passions. It's been promised to me, and I call this promise forward now.

*I'm in control of the choices I make in my life.

*I choose all good, positive feelings over negative ones.

*I choose to replace any negative thoughts or emotions that come up with the positive, opposite ones.

*I choose and deserve to be happy and free from worry, depression, and anxiety.

*I choose kindness over aggression.

*I choose to love and believe in myself.

*I choose to be gentle with and take care of myself.

*I accept all these statements as my truth.

CHAPTER 6

Dealing With Negative Emotions; Stepping Up and Into Your Inner Power

Anger, fear, sadness, shame, regret, pain—they're all real. They come up in us when we least expect them. What to do about these demons that show themselves without warning?

My healing journey involved examining each emotion as it came up over and over again, asking, "What is this? Where did it come from and why is it coming up now?" Identifying the emotion and asking, "What triggered this emotional response in me? Where did I feel it in my body? Why am I feeling this way in this very moment?"

The same thing can be done with illness and any pains in the body.

These are usually tied directly to an emotional response of some sort, some *external* stimuli. Your body will tell you everything you need to know to heal itself. Your job is to go *inside* and ask. After you have identified everything about whatever it is, make peace with the emotion, accepting it for what it is; thanking it for showing up, teaching you what you needed to know about yourself ... then telling it that it's no longer needed now for your highest good. And return it to the light for transformation and healing. It almost magically disappears.

This is an amazing process that does work. It's all about becoming more and more aware of your feelings as they come up. Your emotions and feelings simply want to be felt, acknowledged, and loved. They're doing their job. They are trying to get your attention; they are messengers from your heart and soul, letting you know through your feelings something you need at that time to move forward. Only by looking at them closely and asking what messages they have for you will you really understand why they are there. Mostly, we ignore them and cover them up because they can be painful, and we don't understand what they're trying to get across to us. It's only human nature.

No one wants to look deeply into their fear, hurt,

guilt, shame, and anger. And sometimes the answers do not come immediately. However, just recognizing them, accepting them for what they are, releases them from their pursuit to overcome your mind and eventually affect your body. We must not ignore them, no matter how painful they may be. That definitely will not help the underlying matter at hand. I only know because I've done this many times myself—only to my detriment at the time. I caused myself many years of suffering because of this.

Ignoring them and shoving them back down even further, they begin to stack up. And over time, this can lead to various illnesses and serious diseases. It did me! These emotions must be dealt with on a regular basis. And over time, it becomes easier to recognize them and deal with them right then and there. You will be pleasantly surprised at how this works. It sounds harder than it really is.

The hard part is becoming so self-aware that you catch them coming in. Immediately go through the process I have shared and be ready for the next one. The more you practice this, the less and less negative emotions will flare. They're only messengers relating to you a deeper issue that needs to be resolved.

There is something very powerful in laying them all

out in front of you and just taking them one by one, asking, "What are you trying to tell me?"

As I first started using this method or approach to dealing with my negative feelings and emotions, I would begin to cry, realizing in that moment that which had been lying dormant all those years that I had ignored and buried deep inside of myself. The heart or gut is mainly where they go when being ignored and stuffed, and they don't like it—being stifled.

It's like you are really ignoring yourself; a valid part of your soul is speaking to you in those deep emotions, and we mostly ignore them. That's when the festering occurs. I believe this is the source of so many diseases that we cannot seem to find cures for. And strangely enough, the cures are right there inside us, waiting, begging for our attention before it's too late. No, I'm not a physician, per se. I'm only telling you what I have discovered and has worked for me many times. There is a psychological cause and a biological response to everything and vice versa. The body is simply a mirror image of the mind.

Accepting this could save your life. It did mine. Write a note to yourself and post it somewhere you will continually see it. This is another powerful healing

tool. The note to self reads: "I am allowed and give myself permission, as no one else can, to recognize and heal my negative feelings and emotions; to be free from the need to hang on to this heavy stuff any longer; to become and re-create the person I truly was meant to be now. In recognizing this, I am hereby releasing it all back to you, Spirit, as these things are in the light of my heart and soul now, no longer living in the dark shadows of myself. I choose to *first forgive myself* and then others involved. Starting with me, then my parents, my siblings, exes, kids, people I thought didn't like me and bullied me growing up, or those who I am allowing to control me now.

I choose to release these old worn-out beliefs, emotions, and feelings in a balloon to the Universe for healing and transformation. These feelings no longer serve my highest good, but they certainly got my attention, and I am recognizing the power within me now. I am not defined by my feelings and emotions, my pain of the past; *I am not a victim.*

"I choose to willingly accept the purity of my heart over my mind; the peace, love, and joy that comes from this deep release of what I questioned, once served me, but no longer does. I fully step up and into my power and purpose ... into me. I choose to fully accept the reality of my truth, the me that has

always been there, and embrace the fullness and beauty of who I really am. I choose now to re-create my life's paradigm as the inner alchemist I AM comes to fruition."

CHAPTER 7

Discovering Your
Inner Gems

After years of being raised in an abusive environment, I left home to pursue my undergraduate degrees. Then I later attended law school at age 32 as a single mom. I became a successful attorney, owned a law firm, was at the height of my career, suddenly finding myself fighting like hell to survive breast cancer four times and a mastectomy. Then dealing with the aftermath: including losing my marriage, home, business, career, and self "identity" of who I "thought I was" before. Coming back to life, asking: "Who am I now? Where am I, and why am I here?" Digging through the rubble deep enough to find "me," remembering who I am and that I had been in there all along but hiding in the ashes of my past. All to rise back up, to be here now, to help you do the same. I am grateful for all of it, and I wouldn't

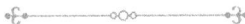

change a thing. I've been where you are. I understand what you're going through, and I share the hidden secrets, revealing a new hope through the "inner resurrection" of you. I'm looking forward to meeting you right where you are. Without any judgment ... we get to choose between being our own worst enemy and being our own best friend.

I have "saved myself" from death, so to speak. Saved from the demons, the emotions from my past paradigm. Coming out of the darkness into the light, cleansed and renewed by self-baptism. I am FREE now at last to step confidently and fully into my once-hidden inner power, the power of me after conquering the fear of the beasts that have been living inside me for so long.

And you can be free of these demons as well. Be willing to go deep inside and look at them, bring them up into the light, examine them, thank them, and release them as we have discussed.

Ask yourself these questions: Who AM I? What are my greatest dreams and aspirations? Am I living my authentic self? What can I change now to put myself back on track to living my truth, purpose, passions, my dreams?

Now is the time! Live one day at a time, taking one baby step at a time. Then ... put on your tool belt and go to task. Go kick some ass and show the world who you truly are!

Although it is true, this chapter is about me, my sacred wisdom journey; my own personal and pro-fessional trials, failures, tribulations, and successes. It is, moreover, for and about you! I wholeheartedly, with sincerity of heart, much pleasure, passion, love, and a true understanding, offer this information with the hopes that it speaks to whatever you might be going through, wherever you are on your life's path, to identify with my life's testimonials on this journey to becoming the authentic, empowered, and amazing being of light that you were meant to BE! To equip you, empower, and inspire you with the tools and the insight I have gleaned throughout the years. To remind you of who you really are and to step into the power of the newly re-created you to do and be what you were put here on earth to become. Living the life of your dreams and greatest aspirations ... to simply BE the best possible YOU that you are capable of being ... To live and be you!

My passion in life is to appeal and identity with you on a heart and soul level. Whether you are going through an illness yourself or with a loved one, grief,

divorce, abuse, self-doubt ... and in general, confusion on what to do and which way to turn next—all of which I have survived and learned and grown from. My journey continues and has been long and winding, exhausting and discouraging at times. It is uphill, downhill, upside down, then right side up. My goal is to recognize and appreciate and see the beauty in everything along the way, to be a better version of myself at the end of every day and to be grateful for all of it.

I have re-educated myself in finding something to be positive and grateful about in every situation along my path ... on my journey to becoming who I am meant to be. The good, the bad, and the downright ugly. It's really beautiful, and each of these bumps has a divine purpose. I have learned the hard way to do what makes me happy, to live my own dreams and passions and not what someone else wanted or expected or tried to change me into being and doing.

To be the best me possible ... to live as the authentic person I am every day of my life.

With that, this is a very condensed version of my life's experiences and lessons. I have only chosen certain parts of my journey to share with you here, which I feel will serve you best to help you "unleash

your own inner superpower!" To become and blossom into who you were created to be!

It is my wish for each of you to be able to take away something, even if only a nugget, that may serve to help and inspire you along your most special and beautiful path we call life ... to rediscover your hidden truths.

Quoting from *The Wizard's Mirror* by Gari Gold Kennedy, a Sedona, Arizona, author, I was struck by a phrase she used that was very profound to me. It was this, "It's about the process, not about the product." And I thought, *That is one of the most perceptive truths I have ever heard, and one which I was never taught. Always caught up in the product, the end result.* But in the series of "supernatural" or "synchronistic" events and occurrences that produce change and spiritual development, we tend to get caught up in the past or in the future and forget to just be in the now. Furthermore, to just "trust the process" is the key.

I realized the very truths in those few words a long time ago, and I began to understand what it means to truly live them. Partially, as in, there are no accidents in this life, and therefore, it is by no coincidence that you are reading these words right now in this very moment on your path. Remember to enjoy the

journey you're choosing; go within and discover your very own beautiful inner gems.

CHAPTER 8

Becoming the Alchemist; Recognizing You Have the Power to Re-Create Your Life

What does success and happiness really mean to you? If you don't know, that's okay; keep reading ...I'm going to spell it all out for you right here and now—because you, my friend, are stronger, more powerful, capable of more success and joy in your life now. You are special, more beautiful, more loved than you now know or can even imagine. Yes, you! Even if you have had success in your life in many areas that you have accomplished on your own ... and for some reason have lost your way, your vision of who you "thought" you were, *your identity*. I know you, too, are reading this. You all already own the strength within to conquer and overcome any obstacles on your path. Some of you are just starting out, and it is great that you are here too. What better time

than now to lift yourself up to learn, grow, stretch, and mold yourself as the alchemist of your life into not only knowing who you are but also what your true purpose, special calling, and passions are for your future and to discover, re-discover, recreate that person—that man or woman.

Most of us as young girls or young men, teenagers, and adults, even as women and men, in today's society, are taught not to think about how unique, special, wonderful, loving, strong, resilient, smart, creative, and truly beautiful we really are inside ourselves. At least that is how I grew up from a very young age. I am a living testimony now, in this very moment, to tell you that it is okay to recognize, feel fully, embrace, be thankful for and love those great gifts and attributes about yourself.

Those qualities and traits that you already possess right now. Not only is it okay, but it is also healthy and necessary for you to know that you can accomplish anything you set your mind to.

However, the question then becomes, how badly do you want it? And that's up to only you. Be patient with yourself, love yourself, believe in yourself. Trust and have faith in the knowledge that you were created to be exactly who you want to become. Feel

it, know it so that you, too, can step into that feeling with confidence, peace, and joy for who you are. Remember, this is a process, and it usually doesn't happen overnight.

Please hear me when I say that sometimes, it's not easy just to believe or know those things are true about you. To fully embrace yourself and your true potential, maybe you even have to have the famous "fake it til ya make it" type of mentality. Soon it will become a knowing deep inside your heart and soul. So rooted in your being that no one can ever take that away from you. Own that one!

Let me regress a bit into my journey, my story through life up to this point. Yes, I have been de-pressed, anxious, scared, alone, lonely, lost, confused, and questioning every single thing about my life. Sometimes asking myself, *Why am I even here? Who AM I? What should I do now? How can I be of greater service? Honor myself, my family, and help others at the same time?*

I AM real. I get it. I know what you are going through. From the top of my head to the tips of my toes ... I know. I have felt many times like giving up. I have felt like it's not worth it. I have felt and believed I'm not worthy, not good enough, not pretty enough.

At my absolute lowest point in life, the actual breaking point of totally giving up, was when it finally hit me. And all of those questions started changing into the realization of who I AM and literally why I have been saved from the clutches of abuse, serious illnesses, bitter heartache, mass confusion, depression, and even death.

From the time I came into this crazy, beautiful world, innocent and pure, the learning began. I grew up in a highly abusive home. Both physically and mentally. I witnessed and experienced it unto myself, as well as to the other members of my immediate family. It was not pretty. There were times I literally thought I was going to die right then in the midst of a battle. Or if not me, I might witness it happening to my mother or one of my two brothers and then have to live with that for the rest of my life. Thankfully and luckily, by the grace of God, I was spared ... we all were. Now bravely bearing throughout life the heavy emotional scarring and learning how to cope with these memories that were stuck somewhere deep inside.

It is not easy to dig deep, to forgive and move on. That subject of forgiveness has its own chapter in another book, but I will touch on the subject briefly, as it is a powerful part of the process of looking deeply at yourself, your paradigms, your emotions and cre-

ating the life of your dreams.

My brothers and I were raised with a heavy hand and taught that formal education is everything and told we had to get this, or we would be a failure and let the family down if we didn't. I now know that education is important but can and does come in many different forms, and I have experienced most all of them.

I went to college, quit after three years, got married for all the wrong reasons at age 21 to find a "new family." Someone to take care of me. I didn't know better at the time ... that's not why you get married! I had recently learned that my father was dying of ALS. A disease better known to many as Lou Gehrig's Disease. And I was a "daddy's girl" despite all of the abuse. I was told at the end of my freshman year in college by my father at 19 years old that he had maybe five years to live, and it would be a slow, horrid, painful death. My family would not only go through this, but we were his caretakers for most of those years as well. It was brutally difficult and heart-breaking to watch my strong, fearless father, only 54 years old at the time, to suffer such a loathsome and debilitating death without dignity. I was horrified, again scarred with these memories for the rest of my life.

I had my only child at age 22, a mere child myself. Out of this failed marriage came one of the greatest gifts of my life, if not the greatest! I had no clue as to what I was doing or how to raise a child, much less one who would grow up to be one of the best of people I know with a huge heart, successful in his own right ... one of the most loving fathers and husbands there can possibly be. The tests and lessons came hard and fast, and I was unprepared mentally, physically, emotionally, and spiritually. I made some critical mistakes, but through it all, we became the best of friends—and still are. We literally raised each other, going through it all together ... just he and I. He has taught me some of my greatest lessons, and I'm so proud and grateful for him.

Two weeks after I divorced his father, my father passed away. One of the saddest days of my life ... even considering the rife and struggle, abuse and sadness that had occurred throughout my life. He had taught me a lot. He was a wonderful encourager to his children, provider for his family, and we knew he loved us and helped form us into who we are today.

He taught us that we could do anything we wanted to do if we set our mind to it. This is something I have passed on to my son, and he is passing on to his

children. For those things, I am grateful to my father and have long since forgiven him.

My son was two years old; I was newly divorced, physically alone for the first time in my life, except for my beautiful child ... with no help to get through it all. I had quit school, and I was totally in the spin cycle. I had a few meaningless jobs, was broke, and totally lost. I soon returned to college and received my bachelor's degrees, sadly leaving my son every day with strangers and paying for school with student loans and working part-time at the school to help with living expenses, groceries, and daycare. That great lesson I was taught from a young age kicked into high gear. I knew I could do anything I wanted to do if I wanted it bad enough and was willing to work hard for it—and I was, and I did just that.

After graduating from college, I worked different sales jobs for eight years until my son was 10 years old, and I was 32, still not remarried. I started questioning what I really wanted to be when I grew up. Who was I now?

The sales profession was not fulfilling for me, but it paid the bills. I had for many years thought I wanted to be an attorney, someone whom my parents would be proud of. I knew I wanted to help people. I ques-

tioned how in the world I could continue to raise my son alone and afford to go to law school and study all night every night. Well, I dug in my heels, decided somehow I could and would just make it work and began the process. I turned the application in on a wing and a prayer, and lo and behold, I, being a single mom at age 32 amongst mainly recent college graduates still living at home with mom and dad, was admitted to law school. It was indeed a very joyful moment in my life. However, it would be a grueling three years of the most intensive long hours and days of reading and studying I had ever done. It was a monumental task I had undertaken. As one out of only 80 students accepted, I was the happiest and most excited person in that classroom on the first day of school. Yet, I very soon began to wonder if I had made a mistake.

We lost 10% of our class in the first two weeks because of the intense workload, pressure, and archaic teaching methods. At that time, there was no turning back. Attending as a full-time day student, none of us were allowed to work a job during the first two years. It was very difficult, to say the least, as I struggled financially to provide for my still-young son, to be both mom and dad to him while attempting to make the grades.

I was determined. I wanted it bad enough. My mind was focused and set, and I did what I had to do and graduated in three years with honors.

In the third year of school, when they admittedly "re-scrambled our brains," wow ... I then started focusing on passing the bar exam and getting a job after graduation. Could I do this after all? That was another wake-up call! What if I didn't pass the bar? And then ... God forbid, what if I couldn't find a job? I used every tool and resource I had learned and gathered from all of my experiences to that point, and truly, miraculously, I did both! It was like every other thing in my life. It was part of my destiny. Another milestone accomplished!

And believe me, I had to use every tool in the box, what I had ever learned about becoming successful and getting what I wanted. And they worked! I believed in myself first and foremost. I didn't give up.

I had faith and persevered. All of the grueling work, the blood, sweat, tears, and many sacrifices would soon pay off.

I went on to become a successful attorney and built from scratch a thriving law firm. I owned two office buildings and had a huge overhead. I was the only

attorney cracking that nut with 8–10 people as my support team. Nothing to sneeze at, but I still didn't feel like I had done something anyone else couldn't do. I knew even then that wasn't it. I knew I had a higher purpose and a greater calling in my life.

Everything was going gangbusters beyond my wildest imagination when suddenly and shockingly, out of nowhere, in the very same year and month after receiving that award, the seemingly impossible occurred. After all I had already overcome and survived to get to that point in my life, I was diagnosed the first time, during a routine mammogram, with DCIS Breast Cancer. What a totally disturbing, completely shocking blow to my system that was!

I was blind-sighted, to say the least. No family history of breast cancer, and when the radiologist who read all of my different test results sat me down to give me this news, as I sat there in alarming disbelief, he looked at me and said, "You look like a deer in headlights." *Wow!* I thought to myself ... *Did you really just say that?* So rude and altogether heartless and dispassionate. I can still hear those words as they burned into my brain. And I relive that moment in my mind to this day so vividly clear.

I was told I needed to do a lumpectomy first and then

radiation for 60 straight days. And I was still trying to work and keep all of the balls in the air. Again, very strong, faithful, unyielding, and positive ...

I had to be through it all.

Eventually, I ended up having to give up everything I owned, including my career, my whole identity, my home, my business, and ultimately the love of my life, whom I had married, shortly after the first diagnosis, treatments, and surgery.

But now, literally, everything else was gone in the history books of my past. The two most important things I could possibly have been left with ... my life and my son, I felt grateful and extremely blessed for. However, I would incredibly be diagnosed and survive three additional diagnoses over the next eight years with recurrent DCIS breast cancer in different stages. I cannot even tell you today exactly how many seemingly unending biopsies, surgeries, tests, and all kinds of procedures with an inevitable bi-lateral mastectomy and reconstruction I have been through. And I continue to endure more procedures, tests, and pain from the mastectomy and recon- struction to this day. It was seemingly endless and extremely difficult, alone and scared to death again. Doctor's appointment after doctor's appointment;

trial after trial; test after test. Immediately following the mastectomy, as if that wasn't enough, I was told I needed to do18 months of chemotherapy! And I knew that, in and of itself, would have killed me. That would have been the final trauma to my body. By that time, I had learned too much.

I declined chemotherapy and told the surgeon right then and there that when it was time for me to move on to the next world, God would have to take me, and I would go. But I was not going to let chemo kill me. Never! That has been almost nine years ago.

Miraculously, I had been spared again!

A note to readers here; these were all very personal decisions I had to make, which I felt best for me at that time. You, if ever faced with a decision similar, must make these decisions for yourself as to what is best for you. Everyone differs in their beliefs, choices, and needs.

Joyfully, I am still alive, thriving in spite of every-thing and doing well—although still always know-ing, in the back of my mind, that cancer could metas-tasize somewhere else in my body at any time.

Once you have had cancer even one time, those

thoughts are there in the back of your mind. It's just something you learn to live with. I stay strong, refusing to give in to the fear or to even entertain this notion and go on doing the best that I can in every moment I am blessed with. Even as the embedded scars and memories still exist, I recognize and acknowledge them for what they are, thank them and release them back to God for transformation into the light, as they are no longer needed for my highest good. Staying in fear is counterproductive. As I released them, I continued learning to live again, UNLEASHING MY OWN INNER SUPERPOWER, going on to becoming the person I was meant to be at this time. Faithful, fearless, and unwavering; more determined than ever, unshakeable ... continuing to reach for and achieve my greatest goals and passions. I am yet again recreating myself. No longer identifying with the successful practicing attorney I was known to be.

I am living out my dreams of having a home on the beach, writing, teaching, speaking ... inspiring and motivating others just like you; bringing this life-altering information to light. I am delighted, grateful, and fortunate to be here now, to briefly tell you my story and to give you the tools that got me through all of this. I'm going to list them as affirmations, as a quick reference guide for you. Write and rewrite

them, recite them aloud, meditate on them, tape them to your bathroom mirror ... whatever you have to do and are comfortable with to remember them.

Never lose sight of you! Pursue your goals, your dreams, with unwavering faith, strength, and determination. Enjoy the journey; write your own movie of how you want to live your life. And stop to smell the roses along the way! You deserve this!

The biggest lesson of them ALL is and always will be to believe in yourself and know in the core of your being that you can and will do whatever it is your heart desires. YOU are all beautiful in your own special way. Stay strong and power-filled in every sense of those words. Become the person you were intended to be. You already have what it takes! Dive deep and deeper inside to find your answers ...that's where they lie ... just waiting on you to find them. Bring them to the surface and into the light. Polish them up and watch yourself shine. You can do this.

From the great motivational speaker and teacher Dale Carnegie in his best-selling book, **How to Win Friends and Influence People,** comes these all-encompassing words. Words I still live by every single day:

"If you think you can't, you won't.
If you think you might, you might.
If you think you WILL, you WILL!"

Never give up on you and your dreams. Know what you want; know you can do it; set your goals; take small baby steps when you need to; believe in yourself! And just go for your deepest, most burning desires; your greatest wishes and the aspirations for your best life. No one else can do it for you.

Have faith and trust in a higher power that is and lives within you.

Know in the depth of your being ... reach deep inside you and reclaim all of the gifts you possess to BE TOTALLY YOU. Rediscover that power-filled person who lies in wait within your soul, waiting to be awakened to that beautiful, strong, loving, dynamic, unique you who YOU truly ARE. Believe in you! Be true to yourself. Live your truth, your dreams, your authenticity ... and watch yourself learn, grow, prosper and bloom into that person of which you already are, who you have been all along, though maybe has been hidden through life's misfortunes, mysteries, defeats, setbacks, and confusion. Believe me when I tell you that you are still in there ... just go in far enough, no matter how deep, and find yourself. You

will love what you find! That's my promise to you.

Congratulations, for the seeds are now planted. All you have to do is water them and watch them grow! A new season of your soul is coming.

Much love and many blessings and good luck on your personal journey to rediscovering you. ALL of you incredibly beautiful, powerful superheroes out there.

Affirmations for Believing
in the Power Of You.

I know that I can do whatever I want to do because I want to do it bad enough.

I'm focused and creating now the life I want. I AM the alchemist.

The Universe is totally supporting me in every way.

I get everything I ask for, believing and seeing in my mind, heart, and soul it is already my reality. It is done.

I love and believe in myself and know in my heart and soul I am worthy and deserve to be happy living my greatest desires and my life's true purpose now.

I AM strong and wise, and I know this to be true. I can do this!

I know that everything WILL and IS always working out for my highest and best good, even if I cannot see how at the time.

I am living each moment of every day as if it were my last; I have no regrets in my life.

I have faith, live and love fully. Laughing just two minutes every day lengthens my life!

I love myself and others unconditionally. I completely forgive myself first so that I can forgive others. I hold no grudges, anger, or fear.

I release any negative thoughts which come up back to the light for healing and transformation.

I am successful and abundant in every way, living my dreams and my greatest aspirations right NOW.

I am living in the now; one day at a time, one minute and every second at a time.

I take baby steps whenever I need to. And put one foot in front of the other. Bravely, confidently walking my path with excitement and joy.

I am enjoying my journey and am grateful for all of the treasures and blessings I am receiving and accepting along this path.

I AM MOVING FORWARD in ALL WAYS AT ALL TIMES, only looking back at the lessons I have learned along the way, for they are my honorable teachers.

EVERYTHING FROM NOTHING

When you expect nothing, you will get everything.

If you expect everything or anything at all ...

you will get what you expected, which is ... nothing.

Expect nothing, and you will be pleasantly surprised that you will, in fact, get everything!

CHAPTER 9

Blind Spot;
Discovering Yours

What's hindering you? No, what is preventing you from seeing, loving, or believing in you? Is it hate, anger, shame, fear, judgment, unforgiveness of yourself or others in your life? What is keeping you blind to who you really are?

Are you refusing to accept the truth of your greatness, your inner power, your own strengths and your ability to succeed? Are you just lost on your path?

Are there some blind spots that you cannot see around? Are they blocking your view from some things that you really need to see?

To have the ability to move forward, you must remove what's keeping you blinded to your own value,

your truths, your wishes, your ability to live the best life possible—the life you were created to live, the life you truly are worthy of and deserve.

If you are questioning your own worthiness, your own abilities, your own Spirit-given light within ... or if that light has diminished and is growing dimmer and dimmer ... and you continue to refuse to accept the truth of who you are, then this chapter is speaking directly to you.

Drop the mask keeping you in the dark and hiding your light, hindering your full vision of your inner power; take a good long look inside your heart and soul. Go deep, then deeper until all your hidden gems of truth are out in the light.

Then you will see the why and you will see through the "blind spots." You actually are hiding from yourself the truth of who you are. We cover up and protect ourselves from being seen fully in our light. We can do this in many ways. A lot of times we bury our light, our authenticity of who and what we really are, so deep within that we can't even see it or even believe it's there. It's hidden in our "blind spots," hiding in the ashes of our past. What has happened in your life that convinced you on such a deep level that you're not good enough; that you're not beau-

tiful, smart, capable, and just plain doomed to be a failure? Are you in pain over it?

If you are using alcohol, drugs, anything to numb this pain and don't know why you're doing it, remember and acknowledge that it only temporarily hides the pain, enabling you to hide behind whatever your drug of choice is. But it is no more than a temporary fix, causing you more pain and sadness overall. It will just get worse and act to keep you in a weakened state, where you are really not happy or fulfilled. It's an illusion created in your mind's eye. A blind spot in your vision, hindering your personal growth, your ability to live your dreams, joy, passions, and purpose.

Is that what you are doing to hide from yourself and everyone else? To squelch your emotions and deny yourself the freedom to shine your light unto the world? Ask yourself, Is this in my highest good? If not ... do the releasing exercise we discussed in depth. Keep repeating it ... keep doing that which releases your old negative habits, emotions, and prior conditioning. It takes 21 successive days to break a habitual behavior. You are letting the mind control you again. That's not the answer. It's not something outside of you; it's all within. Go there! You will find everything you need. Trust me; it's there.

Another way we hide our pain is overeating. Eating your way to happiness is a losing proposition as well. It's, again, a temporary fix, which makes us feel worse in the long run ... we become even more miserable. You are perfect just the way you are. Love your body; treat your body well. Abusing it only serves to keep you stuck in your despair and shame. Learn to just love and accept yourself for everything you are. And you have the tools all right here to find yourself again. To break negative emotions and become "unbreakable." Remember too, you're stronger than you even know.

Are you always feeling like the victim in life? That's another blind spot. You can't see past it because you're stuck in your negative story. You have to force yourself to obtain a different view of your blaming others for all your pain and unhappiness. And only you as the alchemist can make the decision to take another look and consider something different and realize that you and only you can change this programming. Break that old recording; ditch it ... your true happiness and best life ahead depends on this.

There are so many blind spots we create to keep us from being all we can be; to keep us stuck with a weak, pitiful excuse for why we are unhappy. Start

by becoming more self-aware, asking, Where are my blind spots? Then start working on releasing them to the light so you can clearly see the way around them. Using the very same process we have used for everything else. Be brutally honest with yourself. Only you can do this ... no one else can rescue you from you. No one but YOU. How bad do you want it? Do you really want to live your joy? Do you really want to live your dreams, passions, truths, and purpose?

It takes work, yes ... but once that inner flame starts to increase and burn higher, you will be glad you did it. You will feel relieved and so much better you will never want to stop. Then that becomes your drug of choice because you're living your authentic self, the real you ... that's been there the whole time. Believe you can, and you will! If you want it bad enough, get your shovel out and start digging now ... don't wait.

You'll never do it if you wait for the perfect time. It's just another excuse and a lie to keep you stuck.

Who Am I?

Know you're all these things
Believe in you
BE YOU
You're
Love
You're
Heart
You're
Soul
You're
Powerful
You're
Joy
You're
Divine
You're
Amazing
You're
YOU
And you are enough
~
YOU ARE ALL THAT IS.

Charlotte Murphy, author

CHAPTER 10

Do You Have a Key
But Not a Clue?

I woke up today feeling like "death warmed over." In the proverbial fetal position, no less. With one hand clutched, my nails digging into my palm. I had been having a bad dream, really a nightmare, of being on the road to somewhere, not knowing where I was going ... and everything was a mess. Me, my stuff, my car, everything. I had no idea which way to go. In my dream, I had no direction.

I had a key but no clue ... I kept turning on different roads and circling around and around, lost on the very same road with no sense of direction ... no sense of when to turn left or turn right ... just lost ... and I couldn't figure it out. What was really going on inside of me to have this come up out of nowhere?

It was one of the worst feelings I'd ever had. At least not in a long time. And it *seemed* so real

I've always had a pretty good sense of direction, but when it starts getting dark, and you are confused, turned around, feeling literally like you're standing on your head ... nowhere to really call home, no one to call to ask directions, no one ... who do you turn to? I desperately need to know NOW!

"Super Chic" here, just stared in the mirror too. Not only did I feel like "death warmed over," but I also looked like it too ... Oh my God ... my heart racing, what has happened to me? That's not me in the mirror. She doesn't even look like me. She looks 25 years older ... 20 pounds heavier ... wrinkled skin, short hair ... Holy crap!

What had happened to the girl I knew to be me?

I had always fought my weight because my mother, from the day I was born, told my father I was not "her baby" because I was a chubby little ball of a thing. That's the moment it all started.

I've always thought I was too fat ... that makes sense ... never thought I was pretty enough; that makes sense. Never thought I was good enough; that, too,

makes sense …

But why the severe angst about it now? After all the things I've overcome in my life?

That doesn't make sense …

Sometimes, *life just hits us out of nowhere … smack dab between the eyes.*

Panic and fear tightened their grip upon my entire body, mind, and soul. For God's sake, someone help me, please!!! I was having a breakdown right then and there. Tears began to stream heavily down my cheeks …

"Who is this? Who IS THIS?" I screamed repeatedly in the mirror.

I stopped in the middle of the road at daybreak. "Please tell me who you are and what you're doing here in my car with me?" "Why, why, why are you here?" I pleaded for the answers. "I don't know you!" I began to scream at the image which I no longer recognized in the small dimly-lit rearview mirror.

"Damn you, mirror!!!" "Damn everything!" I'm totally lost going the wrong way on a one-way street

too! And NO ONE can help me. Not even "myself" ... that's where I really lost it.

Who IS "myself"? Oh my God ... who AM I?

My mind suddenly went to a meadow with blooming wildflowers and a bright blue sky above. I sat alone on the side of a hill. I was seated, looking around at beautiful scenery everywhere.

There was a gorgeous blue body of water down below, a beautiful valley on one side and rolling hills everywhere I looked. A serene, calm feeling; a sense of peace suddenly came over me. It felt so good just to relax there a few minutes. I leaned my head back and looked up at the beautiful sky. It was a (bluebird) shade of blue, with white billowing clouds floating by. I made angels out of some, animals out of some. And some just appeared as faces staring back at me. I couldn't remember how I even got to this place, but I knew I didn't ever want to leave ... It was so peaceful, and it felt so good to just be able to finally stop and breathe. To be still, rest my mind, and feel my breathing. To close my swollen, red eyes and realize I was safe, even alone, with just me. I was calm, more ... me again.

No mirrors ... with me staring, looking like a deer

in headlights ... no more panic ... it was quiet in my headspace once more ...

I realized I needed nature surrounding me, where I could gather my thoughts in a tangible silence; a place ... that if only in my mind's eye I could wrap myself up in the tapestry of the beautiful landscape before me and feel my body temperature returning to normal.

A boat would be nice on still water somewhere ... although I used to love canoeing the rapids of the rivers in Arkansas ... hmmm, my thoughts were becoming more crystallized. I was once again making sense to myself ... was I actually envisioning a place I would be going? Had I been there before? Or was it all nothing but a dream?

I realized at once, no one had the answers to the questions I was yearning for ... no one but me. I had them all along. And the answers would begin to show themselves because, in the middle of it all, I stopped and asked the Universe, my angels, to reveal to me my own truths ... who *I AM* really IS ...Where have *"I"* been? And where *AM I* going? *And the answers miraculously came ...*

Listening in Silence

I listened in the beauty of the peace
and the silence all around me.
It's in that silence of our souls,
when our minds finally become still ...
that these answers do come.
Out of the dark night of the soul
into the light once more we emerge,
like a caterpillar gaining its butterfly
wings.
Renewed with new freedom to
expand, finally stretch up and out
and fly high into the bluebird skies
from whence they came.
A brand-new Season of Life
to be the beauty, love, and grace of
who and what
they were meant to BE.

Charlotte Murphy, author

CHAPTER 11

Finding Clarity

How did I find myself again amongst the rubble of my background full of pain and heartache? Many, many, harrowing days and nights from a very young age jumping up and down in my day bed, screaming for someone to come get me because I was scared to death. My father and mother in the other room yelling words I couldn't even understand their meaning as of yet ... Why won't someone come get me? I'm hungry ... I'm wet and cold and alone ... in this room ...

And I need help! The same exact way I was feeling this very morning. Although somewhat different because I haven't really eaten anything much in days. I had not been out of the house, except to get absolute necessities. And this time, I realized it wasn't my mother starving me of attention and not feeding me

... no, it was me ...

But why? I asked myself. *Why are you abusing yourself? Is it so ingrained within you that you think that's the way of life? The way or the who someone else told you your life has to be like? The way someone else said you don't deserve better treatment from you?* I reached over and turned the light on. A 2:22 time showed up on my clock the very second I looked at it the first time today. The angels are showing me I'm never alone; they are God's servants, and they had been sent to help me ... yes, it's true. We all do have angels. And that is one of the ways in which they show themselves. But that's another book totally.

This was an aha moment ... an epiphany. It was **me** doing it to myself ... *But again, why?* I continued to ask myself. More visions came of being on the playground alone, no one wanting to play with me ... much less talk to me. Was this my imagination playing tricks on my mind?

My thoughts again returning to those formative days between 1–7 when I was just a baby and being left in my bed. Many, many days, months, and years have gone by since then ... my life as a whole is starting to finally make sense. This is what I've been struggling with ... this is it. The very thing I needed to be able to

say. "Ahhhhh," *now it's all coming together*. The puzzle pieces are starting to fit! I'll be darned but never damned! No matter who thinks differently! I know better. *I know who I AM*. And it feels so good to say that!

Even the kids in the neighborhood didn't want to play with me. Some told me I was funny, that I made them laugh. That made me feel really good. I was funny but not fun? That didn't make sense ... but it started a pattern in my life of just wanting to feel liked by someone, anyone. Not to even mention loved. That word was never spoken in our house. It wasn't a home filled with joy and laughter; it was just a house where we had a bedroom, ate meals, and then went to school and came home to do homework. Only on the weekends did I get to watch cartoons as a little kid. We watched football on Saturday afternoons and John Wayne western movies on Friday night with my dad.

I never heard the words "I love you" said to me or between my parents. No hugging, no good night kisses, no parents holding hands ... none of that stuff. I didn't really even know what love was ... and now, looking back, have I ever really felt loved, really loved by anyone? Have I ever really known how to love myself? How do you teach yourself to love

yourself so you can give love to someone else or to accept love? There have been moments of learning to love myself, but I had to have done something really big to feel like I "deserved" to be loved growing up. And that would be through "doing" something my parents thought was really good, like making high grades or having a teacher brag on me ... What about just loving someone, including yourself, for just who the person is? You or anyone else?

I was rewarded with dinners out at the cafeteria up the street at the mall when I made acceptable grades.

But if I made a C on my report card ... all hell broke loose. One time especially comes to mind very specifically, and it was unbelievably terrifying.

I was in high school. I rode the school bus back and forth because, well, not really sure why—because my mother never worked. And that's beside the point ... But I had feared bringing a report card home once ... for very good reason.

I slowly made it off the bus that day and went inside the house, straight to my bedroom. My mother followed me in because she knew it was "report card day." She demanded to see it.

I slowly dug it out of where I had buried it in my stuff and handed it to her ... I didn't even look at her until she made me ... she immediately went into a tirade. I can barely even stand to recall this in my mind and play it over out loud. But her face at the time is etched in my conscious mind. I can only remember one sentence actually ... she screamed, with every muscle in her tightened, red face ... every vein showing on her long, thin neck. She was screaming so loud ... with such intensity in her voice ... I thought surely even the neighbors or the whole neighborhood heard her. She blasted out, spitting in my face these words ... pointing her finger like a gun at me: "You are going to be a failure!! YOU are ..." OMG! My mind just went totally blank ... I literally cannot remember right now in this moment what those sharp, pointed words even were exactly ... but they were something like this ... as the tears started to flow again down my already-stained cheeks as I began to relive the entire horror scene that afternoon. Recalling the terror, the sheer hatefulness in her shrill voice and in my mind and heart ... I let the tears fall ... then and now. It was akin to this, "You are doomed! Your life is damned to hell! Just wait till your father gets home." And she walked out the door, slamming it so hard it nearly shattered the door frame.

That's close enough; you get the gist ... and she left

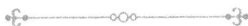

my room, just me sitting alone silent, with just my shivering empty body ... not able to say a word. I lay on my bed with the door to my room shut, crying for hours, alone. And as I stare at the letters here now, on my computer screen ... I hardly know what to say, what to type next ... There are no words to say how I felt then or how I feel now. I do know I was still re-living this pattern of abuse ... not by my parents, a spouse, or a significant other but by me abusing me.

"How does that happen?" you might be asking me ... Even as I have come so far in my life, with no real support ... no encouragement from my mother, tears again start to flow, and I allow them once more. These moments are so very personal to me. I've never even shared any of these stories with anyone. I was too ashamed, too embarrassed, too scared; my soul branded and ripped apart ... even though she is now gone from this earth. And maybe, just maybe, that is what has allowed me to speak the whole truth now. I finally can say I know she loved me in her own way, even though she never said it until the end of her life. I know she did the best she could do or knew how to do. And, of course, I have forgiven her, yet I have not, nor ever will I be able to forget. And I have found a way to see the blessings in every bit of it. These were the beginnings, the making of the ME that you see now. But you, my readers, the people I have

yet to meet, are hearing it because I want to tell you something very important that I learned ... whatever you've been through, whatever you may be going through now ... and even though it may seem impossible for you to believe it yet ... you have what it takes. You have all of the tools necessary right inside you. Yes, you do. I know you may not realize it, but you will ... You, too, are a survivor. You, too, can "rise up" above anything standing in your way.

Believe in yourself.

CHAPTER 12

A Spark of the Divine

There has been much confusion and controversy recently concerning some teachings regarding claims alleging that we are all God. Who would make such a bold and challenging, unorthodox statement and why?

The answer is not exactly clear or precise or easily understood. It involves much personal introspection and understanding. There are the scientific answers, which I do not care to go into, and there is a spiritual answer, which I prefer to focus on in this writing. When you begin to understand who *you* truly are and start to flourish and grow into the full embodiment of your truth, only then can you start to understand. You are a spark of the Divine. And as such, we are all One. Spirit is alive within every single human being.

TRIUMPH THROUGH CHAOS

Strength and clarity come forth from the
darkness;
as light from within, when it is
unexpected;
blinded so that there might be sight;
deafness in order to
hear;
from the depths of within, you suddenly see
clearly;
a death of yourself to be born once
again;
broken-heartedness to heal;
feeling the fullness of love
that surrounds
you.
Ripped apart to restore;
wholeness and richness, life's blessings
adorn.
Stripped naked to welcome
comfort and joy;

finally
rescuing
you;
heart and
soul.

Charlotte Murphy, author

Add furthermore, you are not the body you carry around here. You are not the job or career you have chosen for yourself. And it has been said by many that "you are not a physical being having a spiritual experience, but you are a spiritual being having a physical experience."

What that means is that we can become so involved in our physicality, *who we think we* are in terms of what we do and what we look like, that we become totally consumed and obsessed by these things, and we lose sight of who we truly are. The physical becomes who we are in totality, when in reality it means nothing and will perish with the apple blossoms. Only then to be reborn again into another entity, if we so choose, or body to carry our Spirit forward once more. And *if* we choose to embody some other being, with no recollection of other lifetimes and what we might have learned, only to start all over again, trying to "get it right" this time ... it is an idea that will startle or even be shocking to some, and others may understand. However, it is just an idea, a thought to be reckoned with on a personal belief level for each individual reading this.

I say let's get it right this time! There might not be another time.

Once you grasp this thought, you will begin to shed the peelings, the layers of the onion, one by one, and inside, you will find the lotus blossom in full bloom, waiting to be fully savored by you. It is not an easy process however; it will take some time and can be quite painful. To see who *you* truly are and to dig down to the middle requires an unwavering faith, a commitment, and a yearning for the truth like none other I have ever experienced before. The ego or shadow side of the self usually doesn't like it or appreciate having to give up *its* "identity" as a lawyer, doctor, banker, or whatever *it* calls *you*. This ego usually fights, argues, jumps up and down, and makes a terrible scene as it dwindles slowly away only to reveal your *true* identity—the real you of everything that is in your make-up, the innermost core.

CHAPTER 13

Rediscovering You,
The You You've Always Been

The beauty of the journey lies in our inner power and our inner strength. To take responsibility for ourselves, to our loved ones and to those needing to hear our words through our voices. To be able to stand up and speak our truths, spread our message of "hope through heartbreak" and to pass it on. To pay it forward; to encourage the downtrodden, the abused, the sick, the brokenhearted and lonely to know that they, too, can come through it. And to be an influence, an inspiration, a light in the storm for someone else. It's a very self-healing, self-empowering place to be within yourself. To rekindle the flame in someone else who is lost, confused, fearful, and doubtful. To give hope is to love in the highest form and to the highest degree, not only yourself but those needing it the very most right now. You could be the catalyst

that saves a life, that reawakens someone's dreams and passions and realizes their true purpose. Pass the torch and awaken the Universe. Literally, it's that important and power-filled.

Never tear others down, especially if they're already crawling on the ground. Build them up, remind them who they are, and at the same time, acknowledge who you are. There is nothing I can think of in our world today that is more important or of more value than that. Absolutely nothing compares. This is why I have been spared, allowed so many chances to live. Life is amazing ... live you; you only have one chance in the here and now; this is IT. The time is NOW. Don't wait; just start, even if you don't feel ready. There will never be a better time than in this moment ... of now. That is all we have anyway. If you are waiting for the best time, that time will never come. We are not guaranteed tomorrow—remember that. You matter. Touch someone's soul through a smile, a kind word, an authentic sharing of you. The you you've always been.

WHATEVER YOU'RE TELLING YOURSELF, YOU WILL BELIEVE.

CLOSING

In this book, I am delighted to have had the opportunity to share with you learned wisdom, inner knowing, and truths from the depths of my heart and soul; to have given you some practical tools to take with you and use on your journey within to re-discover and re-align with the truth of who you are. That which always has been and always will be the real and authentic you. You are the answer, my friends, to accept and love yourself in every moment ... no matter what your mind might be telling you. They are all lies as you now know. Lies that hold you back and keep you down. Deception wants to control you, and it will ... but only if you let it. Only you are in the driver's seat now, calling the shots of the new, fulfilled, powerful you, the you that is now re-emerging. The new paradigm for your life.

Remember, you have the power within you to choose a different path. With a new and beautiful view from the heights of brand-new awareness, the consciously awakened you. As you continue on your sacred path, climbing up, up, and up ... rising further up out of the ashes of your past, remember always who you really are; acknowledge your Super Powers, unleash them with your newfound authority, newly gained

control and clarity of you; keep moving forward, up-wards and onwards toward your joy, purpose, goals, and greatest dreams.

Keep pushing and reaching down deeper within yourself, again and again, to go higher than you ever thought you could. Remembering all the while to keep believing in yourself; you are stronger, more powerful, more capable than you ever dreamed pos-sible. You can do anything; never doubt yourself, for you are truly amazing.

Your every scar, your little quirks, imperfections, tics, and idiosyncrasies; they're all beautiful, unique to just you. Love them, they're a part of who you are, and they all add up to the miracle of you. A spark of the Divine ... as we all are.

Your path is uniquely yours, and it's leading you for-ward to always remind you of who you are and why you're here. Reminding you that you have a power-ful purpose for being here; we all do. And you're no exception to this truth.

"We are all ONE with the all that is. Divine, that each one is created differently, yet all with the same spark of light within our heart and soul. The Divinity of oneness of which we are."

Embrace these truths and believe in the power of your very existence. You have been given from birth everything you need right down inside you.

Tap into each feeling or thought, pull it up, examine it for what it is. Ask, "Does this thought, feeling, or emotion serve my highest good?" If the answer is no, hit the delete button; get rid of everything that is no longer serving you and cling to the positive in everything. Being grateful, however, for it all, as every bit of it serves a higher purpose for understanding and determining what is necessary for your growth and highest good. That which is urging you to constantly keep going, no matter what. Never looking back at what was because the past is where it needs to stay; only taking with you the gemstones of truth that serve you now, the lessons you have learned along the way.

Choose to always look for and stay on the positive, bright side; always, always reminding yourself that life is an ongoing process. A process of constant change, re-discovery, learning, and re-creating. And everything—the good, bad, and the downright ugly—happens for a reason. Ask, "What is the lesson in this for me now?" Accept it and deal with it for what it is. Keep putting one foot in front of the other going forward, upwards on your path.

You can do this with faith, hope, and love, and most of all, the powerful belief in yourself and that higher power and inner knowing instilled in you from birth, deep down within you; that knowledge that it's yours, you own, the power of your truths, and nothing, no person, memory, thought, or belief can hold you back now.

Believe and accept these truths as yours in your heart and soul. Step fully into your power and go. Receive your blessings; they are awaiting you.

Thank you for allowing me to share a part of my life's journey, the wisdom of my truths, to help you find yours. I walk this journey with you day in and day out, reminding myself of these very same principles. It is a never-ending process of evolutionary learning and growth. If we think we've learned it all, then we are no longer living. It's a consistent part of everyday life. Although some days we have more clarity than others. We truly are always re-creating ourselves in every moment.

I wish you all of the blessings and goodness in your life that you truly deserve.

I am sending with you the knowledge of your own inner truths and powers; much love, light, and suc-

cess for your happiness and fulfilling joy—for that is your true and Divine purpose.

"Believe, and so shall it BE."
–Charlotte Murphy, author

"Your every thought, your every word,
your every action is a statement to the Universe:
This is Who I Am."
–Neale Donald Walsh

UNSHAKEABLE POWER
Through Seasons of the Soul

By
Charlotte Murphy

www.ingramcontent.com/pod-product-compliance
Lightning Source LLC
Chambersburg PA
CBHW070633150426

42811CB00050B/282